INCREDIBLE FOOTBALL RECORDS

BY MATT SCHEFF

Published by The Child's World®
1980 Lookout Drive • Mankato, MN 56003-1705
800-599-READ • www.childsworld.com

Acknowledgments
The Child's World®: Mary Swensen, Publishing Director
Red Line Editorial: Editorial direction and production
The Design Lab: Design

Photographs ©: ATU Studio/Shutterstock Images, cover, 1, 2; Dick Raphael/Sports
Illustrated/Getty Images, 5; James D. Smith/AP Images, 6; Jack Dempsey/AP
Images/Corbis, 9; Tom Olmscheid/AP Images, 10, 11; G. Newman Lowrance/AP
Images, 12; Al Messerschmidt/AP Images, 16; Martin Jeong/Bettman/Corbis, 19;
Scott Boehm/AP Images, 20

Design Elements: Shutterstock Images

ISBN 9781503808881
LCCN 2015958444

Printed in the United States of America
Mankato, MN
June, 2016
PA02307

TABLE OF CONTENTS

CHAPTER 1

RECORD-SETTING GAMES

MOST POINTS IN A GAME
73 Points
Chicago Bears • December 8, 1940

Seventy-three points. It's the most ever scored by one team in a National Football League (NFL) game. The Chicago Bears did it in the 1940 championship game.

Chicago's Bill Osmanski got the ball in the first minute. He raced 68 yards for a touchdown. The **rout** was on. Chicago scored 11 touchdowns. Ten players reached the end zone. Final score: Chicago 73, Washington 0.

LONGEST GAME
82 Minutes, 40 Seconds
Kansas City Chiefs vs. Miami Dolphins
December 25, 1971

The 1971 playoff game between the Chiefs and Dolphins was one for the ages. Kansas City kicker Jan Stenerud had a chance to win it late. But he missed a **field goal**. That sent the game into **overtime**.

They played 15 more minutes. Still no winner. Finally, Miami scored midway through the second overtime. Dolphins kicker Garo Yepremian ended it with a field goal. At 82 minutes, it is the longest game in NFL history.

GARO YEPREMIAN

LARGEST CROWD
105,121 Fans
Cowboys Stadium • September 20, 2009

The Dallas Cowboys moved into a new stadium in 2009. Their fans could not wait to see it. The stadium had 75,000 seats. Yet 105,121 people squeezed in for the first game. That means more than 30,000 fans watched the game without anywhere to sit!

BIGGEST COMEBACK
32 Points
Buffalo Bills • January 3, 1993

The Buffalo Bills looked dead. They trailed the Houston Oilers 35–3 in the second half of their playoff game. Then backup **quarterback** Frank Reich caught fire. The Bills charged back with 28 points in the third quarter. They even took a 38–35 lead in the fourth quarter. A Houston field goal forced overtime. But then Buffalo kicker Steve Christie booted the game-winning field goal. The greatest comeback in NFL history was complete: Bills 41, Oilers 38.

OFFENSIVE EXPLOSION

The Arizona Cardinals faced the Green Bay Packers in January 2010. Nobody played much defense. The Cardinals won in overtime 51–45. The teams combined for 96 points. That is the most ever in an NFL playoff game.

CHAPTER 2

INDIVIDUAL RECORDS

MOST RECEIVING YARDS IN A GAME

336 Yards

**Flipper Anderson, Los Angeles Rams
November 26, 1989**

Los Angeles Rams receiver Willie "Flipper" Anderson was already having a big day. Anderson caught 8 passes for 171 yards. But the Rams trailed the New Orleans Saints 17–3. Just five minutes remained on the clock.

Anderson was just getting started. He caught a 46-yard touchdown pass. Then his 15-yard touchdown catch tied it. In overtime Anderson capped his day with a leaping 26-yard catch. It set up the game-winning field goal. He finished with 15 catches for 336 yards.

LONGEST FIELD GOAL
64 Yards
Matt Prater, Denver Broncos
December 8, 2013

Playing in Denver can be a kicker's dream. The ball really carries in Colorado's thin mountain air.

Broncos kicker Matt Prater knew that. He trotted onto the field in a 2013 game against the Tennessee Titans. Three seconds remained in the first half. The ball was just past midfield. His kick sailed 64 yards. It split the uprights. His kick was 1 yard longer than the old record.

MATT PRATER

9

MOST RUSHING YARDS IN A GAME
296 Yards

Adrian Peterson, Minnesota Vikings
November 4, 2007

Adrian Peterson's record day started quietly. He had just 43 yards in the first half. But Peterson was unstoppable in the second half. He darted around San Diego Chargers defenders. He bowled right over tacklers.

He was just 3 yards shy of the record in the closing minutes. Peterson took one last **handoff**. He blasted forward for 3 yards, right into the NFL record book.

LONGEST PLAY
109 Yards

Tie: Antonio Cromartie, San Diego Chargers
Cordarrelle Patterson, Minnesota Vikings

Adrian Peterson was not the only one to set a record in that 2007 Vikings-Chargers game. Minnesota came up short on a long field goal attempt. San Diego defensive back Antonio Cromartie caught the ball in the back of the end zone. He ran it all the way back for a touchdown.

Minnesota's Cordarrelle Patterson matched that mark in 2013. He returned a kickoff 109 yards. It's a record that can never be broken.

ANTONIO CROMARTIE

DERRICK THOMAS

MOST SACKS IN A GAME
7 Sacks
Derrick Thomas, Kansas City Chiefs
November 11, 1990

Derrick Thomas was a one-man wrecking crew. The Kansas City Chiefs were locked in a battle with the Seattle Seahawks. Time after time, Thomas blasted through the line. He battered Seattle quarterback Dave Krieg for a record seven **sacks**.

Yet it was not enough. The game went to overtime. Thomas nearly sacked Krieg an eighth time. But Krieg escaped and threw the game-winning touchdown pass.

MOST PASSING YARDS IN A GAME
554 Yards

Norm Van Brocklin, Los Angeles Rams
September 28, 1951

In 1951 Norm Van Brocklin was fighting for the Rams' starting quarterback job. Then teammate Bob Waterfield suffered an injury. Van Brocklin was in.

He made it count. Van Brocklin piled up a stunning 554 passing yards in a game against the New York Yanks. The record has stood ever since.

CARRYING THE TEAM

On November 28, 1929, the Chicago Cardinals beat the Chicago Bears 40–6. **Fullback** Ernie Nevers scored every one of the Cardinals' points! Nevers scored six touchdowns. He also kicked four extra points. No player has ever scored more in one game.

CHAPTER 3

TEAM RECORDS

MOST POINTS IN A SEASON
606 Points
Denver Broncos • 2013

Quarterback Peyton Manning led an unstoppable Broncos offense in 2013. Manning threw a record 55 touchdown passes.

Denver was chasing the New England Patriots' record of 589 points. Manning threw a 63-yard touchdown pass to Demaryius Thomas to break the record. Denver finished with 606 points. That's almost 38 points per game.

FEWEST POINTS ALLOWED IN A 16-GAME SEASON
165 Points
Baltimore Ravens • 2000

With **linebacker** Ray Lewis leading the charge, the Ravens' defense was smothering in 2000. Opponents could barely move the ball at times. Baltimore allowed just over 10 points per game that season.

The Ravens' D was even better in the playoffs. Their opponents scored just 23 points in four games! And seven of those came on a kickoff return. That's one way to win a **Super Bowl**.

PERFECT

In the Super Bowl era, only one NFL team has had a perfect season. The 1972 Miami Dolphins won all 17 games they played. That included a Super Bowl victory.

MOST SUPER BOWL TITLES
6 Titles
Pittsburgh Steelers

No team has had more Super Bowl success than the Steelers. It started in the 1970s. A crushing defense nicknamed "The Steel Curtain" led the way. Pittsburgh won four Super Bowls from 1974 to 1979. In the 2000s, strong-armed quarterback Ben Roethlisberger led the team to two more. Their six Super Bowl trophies are the most in the NFL.

LONGEST LOSING STREAK
26 Games
Tampa Bay Buccaneers • 1976–77

The Tampa Bay Buccaneers had a rough start. The Bucs entered the NFL in 1976. They did not score a point in their first two games. Tampa Bay went 0–14 in that first season.

The losing continued in 1977. By December, the streak stood at 26 games. Finally, on December 11, the Bucs came through. They thumped the New Orleans Saints 33–14. The win snapped the longest losing streak in NFL history.

WINLESS

The 2008 Detroit Lions went 0–16. They are the only NFL team to go winless over a 16-game schedule.

CHAPTER 4

CAREER RECORDS

LONGEST CAREER
26 Seasons
George Blanda

Pro football is a rough sport. Injury and age force many players from the game early. But not George Blanda. He played a record 26 pro seasons.

Blanda's career was unlike any other. He was a star quarterback. But he also was a kicker, a punter, and even a linebacker at times. Blanda was 48 years old when he finally retired after the 1975 season.

MOST RECEIVING YARDS
22,895 Yards
Jerry Rice

Most NFL experts call Jerry Rice the greatest receiver in history. Rice entered the league with the San Francisco 49ers in 1985. Over the next 20 years, he rewrote the NFL record books. Rice became the NFL's top pass-catcher in every major category. That includes 1,549 catches, 197 receiving touchdowns, and 22,895 receiving yards.

JERRY RICE

BRETT FAVRE

MOST CONSECUTIVE STARTS
297 Games
Brett Favre

Crushing hits. Knee-buckling tackles. Twisted ankles. Football is a rough game. And the quarterback is the center of the action. That makes Brett Favre's record of 297 straight starts even more amazing. From September 1992 to December 2010, the iron man did not miss a single game. He also won three NFL Most Valuable Player (MVP) trophies along the way.

MOST COACHING VICTORIES
347 Victories
Don Shula

Don Shula enjoyed a seven-year career as a player in the NFL. But he made his mark on the sidelines. Shula coached for 33 years with the Baltimore Colts and Miami Dolphins. He won 347 games while losing just 173 and tying 6 over that time. He also won two Super Bowls with Miami.

10 STRAIGHT

Otto Graham was one of a kind. From 1946 to 1955, the Cleveland Browns quarterback led his team to the league championship game every year. The Browns went 7–3 in title games.

field goal (FEELD GOHL): A field goal is a kick from the field that goes through the uprights. Garo Yepremian won the NFL's longest game with a field goal.

fullback (FUL-bak): A fullback is a player whose main jobs are blocking, catching passes, and running with the ball. Ernie Nevers scored a lot of points as a fullback.

handoff (HAND-off): When the quarterback gives the ball to a runner it's called a handoff. Adrian Peterson set the NFL rushing record after taking a handoff.

linebacker (LINE-bak-ur): A linebacker is a player who starts most plays between the defensive linemen and the defensive backs. Ray Lewis was a great linebacker for the Ravens.

overtime (OH-vur-time): When the score is tied after four quarters the game goes into overtime. The Bills needed overtime to complete their comeback against the Oilers in 1993.

quarterback (KWOR-tur-bak): The quarterback runs the offense. Norm Van Brocklin set a record no quarterback has matched.

rout (ROWT): A rout is a one-sided victory. The Bears beat Washington in a rout in the 1940 NFL Championship game.

sack (SAK): When the quarterback is tackled behind the line of scrimmage it's called a sack. Derrick Thomas was Kansas City's sack master.

Super Bowl (SOO-pur BOHL): The Super Bowl is the NFL's championship game. The Steelers have won the Super Bowl more times than any other team.

IN THE LIBRARY

Bryant, Howard. *Legends: The Best Players, Games, and Teams in Football*. New York: Philomel Books, 2015.

Nagelhout, Ryan. *Football's Greatest Records*. New York: PowerKids Press, 2015.

Rausch, David. *National Football League*. Minneapolis, MN: Bellwether Media, 2015.

ON THE WEB

Visit our Web site for links about football: **childsworld.com/links**

Note to Parents, Teachers, and Librarians: We routinely verify our Web links to make sure they are safe and active sites. So encourage your readers to check them out!

INDEX

ABOUT THE AUTHOR

Matt Scheff is an author and artist living in Alaska. He enjoys mountain climbing, fishing, and curling up with his two Siberian huskies to watch sports.